Poems by
Elli Woollard

Perfectly
PECULIAR
pets

Illustrated by
Anja Boretzki

BLOOMSBURY EDUCATION
LONDON OXFORD NEW YORK NEW DELHI SYDNEY

Contents

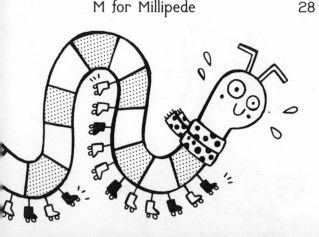

Perfectly Peculiar Pets

Houses make good habitats

For puppy dogs and tabby cats

For guinea pigs and little mice;

Fluffy, friendly, cute and nice.

But why not get a different pet,

The sort to make your parents shout,

To make them faint or tear their hair

And whisper weakly 'Get it out!'?

They sometimes snap, they

  sometimes squeeze,

They cannot sit and be ignored.

But get a pet like one of these,

And you will never once be bored.

A
for Armadillo

I've got an armadillo that I bought in
    Amarillo
Which I pop upon my pillow when I
    snuggle up in bed.
I call her Madam Mandy as she's super
    fine and dandy,
And she's very, very handy when I've
    ants upon my head.

B

for Bison

If you've got a basin and a load of old
   shampoo,
And you are feeling rather bored and
   don't know quite what you should do,
Then go and get a bison, and everyone
   will stare
When you put some little bows on all
   its freshly blow-dried hair.

C

for Crocodile

Happy chappy, snappy chappy,
Snip snip snipping.
Happy chappy, snappy chappy,
Clip clip clipping.
You'll never once need scissors if you've
   got your own pet croc,
Though when silly people see him they
   might sometimes get a shock.

D

for Dromedary

Humpy, lumpy, cross and grumpy,
Not very good for a friend.
But dromedaries taken for walks in the park
Will spice up a sandpit no end.

E

for Elephant

My elephant's a perfect pet;
Nothing could improve her.
As when my room is full of junk
Her trunk's a brilliant hoover.

F

for Flamingo

A flamingo is great for my grandpa
   all right;
They go and play bingo on Saturday
   night.
My grandpa's amazing! How many
   old men go
With flirty flamingos to dance the
   flamenco?
They flit round the dance floor,
   flamboyantly dressed.

But bingo's the thing that they both
   love the best.
And when they're together they
   constantly win, so
I'm happy my grandpa can take
   my flamingo.

G

for Gorilla

I go to the shop and I say 'One vanilla
And two raspberry ripple ice creams'.
But the shopkeeper stops when he spies
  my gorilla,
And then, very strangely, he screams.
'An ape! Escape!' the customers cry,
As they all start to panic and flee.
And then it's just me and my pet (don't
  know why!)
So we both eat our ice creams for free.

H
for Hippo

My hippo's only happy when he hops.
When he dances and he prances and
   he bops.
He loves the mud and muck
That my parents say is yuck,
So I really hope my hippo never stops.

I

for Iguana

Flick–a–lick, flick–a–lick,
Quick quick quick!
Flick–a–lick, flick–a–lick
Slick slick slick!

My mum says that poking your
   tongue's impolite,
But me and Iguana, we do it all night.

J

for Jackal

If you tackle
My jackal
His snack'll
Be you.

You can give him a tickle;
A tickle that's quick'll
Make Jackal behave
And he might even sit.

Or to make Jackal chuckle
A roll in the muck'll
Do wonders for making him
Smile, for a bit.

But a thwack or a whack'll
Be dreadful for Jackal
So never attack him,
Whatever you do.

For if you dare tackle
My lovely pet jackal
I know for a fact
That his snack'll be you.

K

for Kookaburra

My old folks
Make dreadful jokes;
I never laugh
At what they've said.
And so I've got
A kookaburra;
He's the one
Who laughs instead.

L

for Leopard

My cat is charming, long and lean,
The coolest cat you've ever seen.
She likes to curl up on my lap
And close her eyes, and have a nap
While I admire her spots (a lot),
And play a game of dot-to-dot.
But please don't stroke her – don't, I said!
Oh dear, oh dear, where IS your head?

M

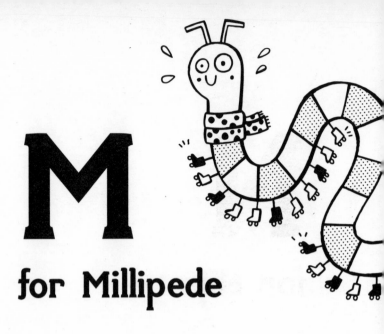

for Millipede

My millipede, my millipede (I call him
   little Billy Deed),
He goes along at silly speeds, on tiny
   roller skates.
My millipede, my millipede (he wears a
   scarf of frilly tweed),
You can't impede my millipede, and that's
   why we're best mates.

N

for Nits

Forget your dogs! Forget your mogs!
Forget your fish and your ferrets
  and frogs!
The best of pets you could possibly get
Are the ones that you'll never have
  thought of, I bet.
Wherever you go, they go there too.
You're always together, your pets
  and you.

I've hundreds! I've thousands! I love
them to bits!
And so, would you like some? Come
here, have some nits.

*Strictly speaking, nits aren't animals at all – they're
the dead shells of eggs laid by head lice.

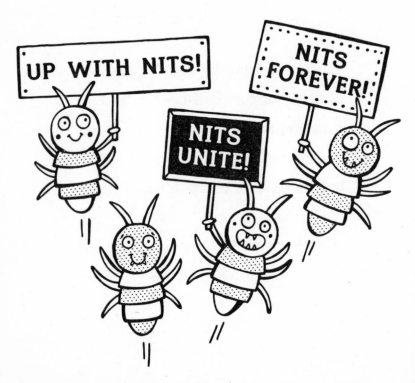

O

for Octopus

An octopus seems a peculiar pet,
But don't be concerned; have no fears,
As strung from the ceiling I've got a
  strong feeling
They make rather good chandeliers.

P

for Platypus

Lazy old mattypus
Greedy old fattypus
Silly old scattypus
Crazy old battypus
Scruffy old tattypus
Splish splosh splattypus
He's one of a kind,
My playful pet platypus.

Q

for Quokka

My parents got a shocker when I first
  brought home my quokka,
And they cried 'Good gracious
  gumdrops! What is that?
Muzzle it (don't nuzzle it), and put it
  in a locker!
It's a hairy scary rodent; it's a rat!'.

But they didn't know my quokka is a
  roller and a rocker
And is great at playing riffs on my
  guitar.
She goes for strolls, and scores the
  goals whenever we play soccer,
So me and my pet quokka, we'll go far.

* Not many animals begin with a 'Q', and you may have
never heard of a quokka. Once thought to be giant rats,
they are in fact marsupials like kangaroos, and live
on an island called Rottnest ('rat nest') Island off the
coast of Western Australia, where some of my family
originally come from.

R

for Rhino

I know
My rhino
Has quite
A strange look,
But for clothes
That I've worn
Then her horn's
A good hook.
I never
Need hangers

Or holders
Or pegs,
As my rhino's
A wardrobe
That stands on
Four legs.

S

for Slugs

Can you smuggle six slugs in
  your sweater
And stroke all their lovely soft slime?
Then juggle the slugs, and jiggle
  the slugs,
Maybe all six at a time?
Can you snuggle six slugs in
  your duvet,
And lie next to them all the
  night through?

Do you adore them and bow down
  before them,
Or do you just simply go
  'ewwwwwwwwwww!'?

T

for Toucan

I've not got a threecan, or fourcan,
    or fivecan,
Or sixcan or sevencan eight.
And though a new onecan would be
    plenty of fun,
I can tell you – my toucan is great!

U

for Umbrellabird

It really doesn't matter if the rain goes
   pitter patter
With a splitter and a splatter and
   a splosh.
With a bird as your umbrella you will
   look quite simply stellar
And you'll make your neighbours
gawp and say 'Oh gosh!'.

V

for Vulture

I'm certain my vulture is into
  high culture
Like opera and music and dance.
And I'm sure that at night when she's
  quite out of sight
Then she spins pirouettes with a prance.

It may not be nice

That she eats long–dead mice,

And she gobbles up flesh

That's a little un–fresh,

And all mouldy and rotten

And green and forgotten...

I'm sure, though, my vulture is into
   high culture

Like opera and music and dance.

She's really quite good; she's just
   misunderstood.

So please will you give her a chance?

W

for Whale

My neighbours don't seem very fond
Of what I keep inside my pond.
In fact, they all turn deathly pale
Each time they see my killer whale.

So when I want to have a swim

The pet I take, of course, is him.

We splish and splash and splosh;
    it's cool

Just two of us, inside the pool.

* Killer whales are very badly named. In actual fact they
are a type of dolphin, and they are unlikely to kill you
unless you happen to be a fish.

X

for ?

I don't know what it is.
My brother says it's his.
I've stroked it and I've poked it
And I've done all sorts of tests
    and checks,
But still I don't know what it is
And so I think I'll call it 'X'.

Y

for Yak

My yakketty Yak won't stop yakking.
My yakketty Yak won't stop snacking.
But his wonderful wool is simply
  the best,
When knitting pink knickers or socks
  or a vest,
And his sweaters are better than all
  of the rest,
So my yakketty Yak gets my backing.

Z

for Zebra

When my parents saw the stripes
They said 'Good heavens, child!'
  and 'Cripes'
'Our three-piece suite will be
  quite wrecked!'
And other words to that effect.
But Zebra's good for pulling loads,
And when I want to cross big roads
But can't find any traffic light,
My zebra's mighty fine, all right!

She stamps her feet, her mane
  starts tossing,
Then she makes my zebra crossing.

So, are you ready to write a poem?

If you want to write poems,
Here's what to do:
Find a clean page
That's lovely and new.
Make it all smooth,
Grab a good pen.
Now chuck them over your shoulder and then...
Stand on your head.
Spin round and round.
Wiggle your nose.
Put both ears on the ground.
Listen to colours.
See every smell.
Touch every sound
And taste it as well.
Take your brain for a jog.
Juggle your thoughts.
Jump with ideas
And words of all sorts.
Fly with your feelings
Up like a kite!
Now you're a poet
And ready to write.

Of course, you don't *really* have to stand on your head and do all this before writing a poem (which is probably a good thing, because I *can't* stand on my head. Can you?) But what you *must* do is give your thoughts and ideas a bit of exercise. You won't write a poem if your ideas are sitting slumped in your brain like lazy couch potatoes.

'Er? What's this crazy poet person on about?'

Let me explain...

Poems very often involve seeing things in a different way. Close your eyes for a minute. Imagine that it's a hot day, there's a gentle breeze blowing, and you see some trees.

Are your eyes closed? NO CHEATING! You *must* be cheating, otherwise how could you be reading this? Ha, ha, caught you out!

But say your eyes were closed, and you *did* imagine those trees. What are those trees doing?

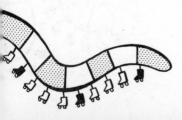

'Nothing. They're trees! Duh!'

I bet though that in a gentle breeze, the trees would be waving about a bit. Or maybe they're not waving, they're… dancing! Are they in a ballet, perhaps? Are they on the dance floor busting their hot moves? And where's the music? Maybe some birds are singing. Or maybe, on a warm day, the sun is *beating* down. Maybe the trees are boogieing to the beat of the sun.

And then from that thought, you could write a whole poem about the trees dancing. Are they good dancers? Rubbish ones? Could they win a TV talent show? You're the poet, you can decide!

That's what I mean about exercising ideas and seeing things in a different way. And *that* is the beginning of poetry.

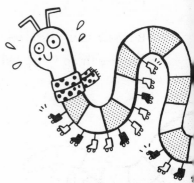

Over to you

OK, now you try seeing something in a different way. If you're stuck for ideas, I'll give you one. How about a table?

'A table? That's boring!'

Is it? Tables have legs, don't they? And what might a table do with legs? What do people do with their legs (might tables play sport, for instance)? What do people wear on their legs? What other objects have legs?

See if you can think of what a table might do with its legs, when nobody is looking.

(There's a fancy-pants word for describing things as if they're like humans. It's called anthropomorphism – *an-thro-po-mor-fism*. Try impressing your teacher with that! But your table doesn't have to be like a human. It could be a dog, for instance, or a dinosaur.)

Yeah but, yeah but...

'But that's not a poem! You're supposed to be telling me how to write poems!'

You're right. There are a few tools that poets use, apart from exercising their ideas. A lot of these tools involve playing with words.

'How can you play with words? They're not footballs!'

Actually, you probably could write a poem about words being footballs! But anyway...Here are a few ways in which poets play with words:

1) Rhyme. Poems don't have to rhyme, although the ones in this book do. Why? It's fun! Thinking of rhymes often help you think of a poem. Does a mango dance the tango? Does a goat eat a boat? Does a cook bake a book? Have a go, and see what you can come up with!

2) Using words that sound similar. If you look at my 'Bison' poem, for instance, you'll see that I use the words 'bison', 'basin', and 'bows on'. Can you see that these all have a similar sound?

(Here's another fancy-pants word for you: alliteration – *a-litter-ray-shun*. All this means is using words that start with the same sound, like slow slimy slugs). Take your name. What words start with the same letter? Are there words that sound similar?

(You might be able to use rhyme with your name too. I am 'Smelly Elli eating jelly watching telly in a welly', just so you know.)

3) Using rhythm. A lot of poems have a beat. You can clap to poems! You can stamp to them! You can dance to them!

'I don't like poems. I like hip-hop music though'

Actually, they're not that different!

See where the beats come in my 'Elephant' poem:

An ELEphant's a PERfect pet,

NOTHing could imPROVE her,

As WHEN my room is FULL of junk

Her TRUNK'S a brilliant HOOver.

That's a very simple rhythm, but some poems have rhythms that are much more complicated. See what you can do, and then dance along to it (or make your teacher or parents do the dance instead. Ha ha)!

Poets have other tools up their sleeves too. These are just some to begin with. So go on, start writing!

'Can I stop standing on my head yet?'

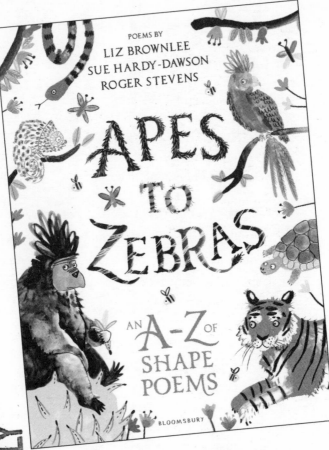

POEMS BY
LIZ BROWNLEE
SUE HARDY-DAWSON
ROGER STEVENS

APES TO ZEBRAS

AN A-Z OF SHAPE POEMS

BLOOMSBURY